St Isaac's
Cathedral

St Is
Cath

SMART

GEORGHY BUTIKOV

aac's
edral
Museum

LENINGRAD

Compiled and introduced by Georghy
Butikov
Translated from the Russian by Elena
Bessmertnaya
Photographs by Alexander Kashnitsky
(interiors)
Designed by Alexander Lobanov
Edited by Tatyana Mamayenko (Russian
text) and Nora Andreyeva (English
translation)
Documentary photographs from the
archives of the Museum of St Isaac's
Cathedral, Leningrad

ISBN 5-7078-0106-5

The Design: A Review of Its History

The Cathedral is St Petersburg's fourth church to be dedicated to St Isaac the Dalmatian, a legendary Byzantine monk. The building of each of the four churches was closely linked to the history of the city, and each of them reflected to some extent its architectural, artistic and town-planning traditions from the early eighteenth century to the first half of the nineteenth.

When Peter the Great founded St Petersburg in 1703, he decided to build in his new capital a cathedral dedicated to St Isaac the Dalmatian whose feast day fell on 30 May, Peter's own birthday.

Several years later, in 1707, a small wooden church was erected on the Admiralty Green. Its modest architecture was in keeping with the first buildings of the Petrine period. On 19 February 1712 Peter and Catherine had their public wedding there. Unassuming as it was in design and decoration, this church soon was felt to be out of keeping with the grand scale on which Russia's new capital was being built. On 6 August 1717 the foundations were laid for a second Church of St Isaac on the bank of Neva where the equestrian statue of Peter the Great ("Bronze Horseman") now stands. This church was designed by Johann Mattarnovi. Peter himself took part in the foundation ceremony.

The site selected for the church proved unsuitable: the ground on the unfortified Neva bank began to shift, causing cracks in the building's walls and vaults. The work of destruction was completed by a fire in May 1735.

On 15 July 1761 the design and construction of a new St Isaac's church was entrusted by a special decree of the Senate to Savva Chevakinsky, who was the architect of the Cathedral of St Nicholas of Myra, which stands to this day. This gifted architect, however, was not destined to carry out his design. Catherine II, who came to the throne in 1762, approved of the idea of rebuilding the cathedral which was linked with the name of Peter the Great and agreed with the site chosen by Chevakinsky; but she entrusted the task of planning and building the new church to another architect, the famous Antonio Rinaldi, often called "master of marble façades". According to his design, the new cathedral was to have five cupolas of elaborate shape and a tall bell-tower; a marble facing was to lend a special touch to its four façades. The building could have become one of Rinaldi's finest creations, but the work moved so slowly that he left St Petersburg before it was completed.

After the death of Catherine II in 1796 Paul I, dissatisfied with the slow rate of progress, instructed the architect Vincenzo Brenna to complete the work with all possible speed. This compelled Brenna to distort Rinaldi's design. The result was a rather squat building with one dome instead of five cupolas. This cathedral was felt to be so much out of harmony with the capital's majestic image that seven years later the question of its rebuilding was raised by the Holy Synod.

In 1809, shortly before the War of 1812, a contest was held in St Petersburg for the best reconstruction design for St Isaac's Cathedral. The terms which had been approved by Alexander I, stipulated that a method should be found to decorate the cathedral without covering

Bell-tower: a tower either free-standing or surmounting a church that supports or shelters a bell or bells

7

up its rich marble facing. Another condition was that the design of the dome should lend "grandeur and beauty to so famous a building". The emperor also wanted "a convenient means of embellishing the Cathedral square, one that would give regular proportions to its area".

Taking part in the contest were Andreyan Zakharov, Andrei Voronikhin, Vasily Stasov, Giacomo Quarenghi, Charles Cameron, and other prominent architects of the time. The contest proved futile because the architects suggested demolishing the old cathedral and building a new one. The emperor took this as "an offence against the memory of the Cathedral's founders", and insisted that part of the old church, namely the sanctuary, should be incorporated in the new building.

In 1816, Alexander I finally decided to start the rebuilding of St Isaac's Cathedral without further delay. He asked Augustin Béthencourt, who was Head of the St Petersburg Committee for Public Construction and Hydraulic Works, to draw up a plan for the rebuilding and to find an architect who could be put in charge of the work. Béthencourt recommended Auguste Ricard de Montferrand, a young architect who had completed with distinction a course of studies at the Ecole Royale et spéciale d'architecture in Paris, and had had some practival training at the studio of the famous French architects Charles Percier and Pierre Fontaine.

In 1816, Montferrand came to Russia where he was to spend the greater part of his life, becoming with time one of the most prominent architects of his age. His undisputed talent, combined with a passion to perfect his mastery of architecture and building techniques, enabled Montferrand to direct this grandiose project for more than forty years, despite occasional setbacks and failures. His method of work was largely dependant on his ability to estimate and make use of the available experience and the technical solutions suggested by many architects, engineers, sculptors and painters.

Philip Wiegel, who directed the office of the Committee for Public Construction and Hydraulic Works, later wrote that in response to Béthencourt's offer to tackle the design of St Isaac's Cathedral, Montferrand produced twenty-four beautiful project drawings for the cathedral, executed in a wide range of styles, from those of classic Greece and Rome, Romanesque and Gothic to Oriental ones.

In a letter to his teacher Percier, Montferrand wrote: "Soon after my appointment as Architect to the Court, I was commanded to take charge of the rebuilding of the cathedral. Designs... had been drawn up at the Emperor's order during all of the fifteen previous years... I thought it would be prudent to find out about the taste of my patron before commencing the work, and made a number of widely diverse sketches."

Montferrand's drawings were submitted to Alexander I. The emperor was so pleased by their artistry and graceful execution that a special decree followed soon, appointing Montferrand Court Architect. He was entrusted with drawing up reconstruction design for rebuilding St Isaac's Cathedral, but the emperor's original decision to incorporate into the new building the sanctuary of the old church stood firm.

Montferrand complied with these instructions. His design, evolved in 1818,

Pier: a solid support that is rectangular in plan

Portico: covered colonnade usually at the entrance of a building

Column: a pillar, circular in plan, consisting of base, shaft and capital

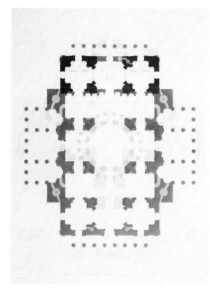

Plan of St Isaac's Cathedral

provided for the incorporation of the building's sanctuary and of the piers that supported the dome. The western wall of Rinaldi's Church was to be demolished but the southern and northern walls would be preserved. In this way only the length of the church would be increased, its width remaining unchanged. The new cathedral would be rectangular in plan and the vaults would be of the former height. Porticoes of Corinthian columns were to be raised on the northern and southern sides. The building was to be crowned by a massive central dome and to have four corner cupolas. A marble facing for the interior walls was envisaged; paintings and sculptures were to decorate the vaults.

The two city squares dominated by the new edifice, St Isaac's and Senate Squares, were also to be redesigned.

After the general plan had been approved, the old cathedral was fenced off, the necessary auxiliary buildings were put up, and the dismantling was started.

On 26 June 1819 the founding of the new (fourth) cathedral dedicated to St Isaac was celebrated with due ceremony. The foundation stone, a piece of granite with a plaque of gilt bronze affixed to it, was laid on top of the piles on which the structure was to rest. Inscribed on the plaque was the date of the beginning of the new project. Construction work was soon started.

In effect, Montferrand received this commission because not one of the noted architects was willing to jeopardize his official standing and professional reputation.

Soon, however, strong criticism of Montferrand's plan came from Auguste Mauduit, the French architect who held the high office of member of the St Petersburg Committee for Construction and Hydraulic Works. In October 1820, he presented to the Academy of Arts a memorandum with his critique of Montferrand's design.

Mauduit's objections ran along three basic lines. He doubted the reliability of the foundation and its capacity to carry a building of such great weight; he predicted the danger of a non-uniform settling of the structure's old and new portions; last but not least, he pointed to the defective design of the dome whose diameter exceeded the tolerance limits, and this was fraught with the danger of its crumbling – especially because it would rest on piers of different date.

To these architectural points Mauduit added some disparaging comments of a personal nature, accusing Montferrand of professional incompetence as architect and builder. Count de la Ferronet, the French Ambassador in Russia, thought that Mauduit was jealous of his compatriot's success. Trying to discredit Montferrand, Mauduit sent several incriminating letters to the emperor. The whole matter gained wide publicity in St Petersburg.

On 21 October 1820 Mauduit's memorandum was discussed at a meeting of the Academy of Arts members, who agreed with one voice that the matter was of the greatest importance and deserved close consideration. The Academy's conclusions were submitted to the emperor. A special committee was formed "to look into the remarks of the architect Mauduit concerning the rebuilding of St Isaac's Cathedral". Among the committee members were noted architects and engineers, such as Alexei Olenin, President of the Academy of Arts; the Mikhailov brothers; the architects Rossi and Stasov; the stone-masonry expert Rudzha; and the engineers Basen and Destrem. Mauduit's memorandum was handed to Montferrand, who was told to

St Isaac's South Façade According to the 1825 Design. Lithograph after a drawing by Auguste Montferrand. 1845

ÉLÉVATION GÉOMÉTRALE DE L'ÉGLISE

present "detailed explanations".

Work on the construction site was halted. The committee studied Mauduit's critique and Montferrand's explanations.

Trying to clear his name, Montferrand wrote in the explanatory note addressed to Alexander I: "To refute the slander disseminated by competitors who want to picture this architect as a mere draughtsman, I beg leave to remind you that during my six years in Russia I have built more than my critics." Montferrand defended his original design, stating his own conclusions and citing examples from the general history of architecture; he supported his theoretical propositions by a detailed description of the work implemented so far. As a result, some of the charges against him were dismissed – including the most important point about the cathedral's foundation. Montferrand affirmed his full awareness of the problems posed by the incorporation of portions of the older building; but, being constrained by the proportions of the old church, he had not been able to increase the spacing between the supporting piers so as to match the increased diameter of the dome.

In his explanatory note to the committee Montferrand again stressed his deference to the emperor's wish: "Out of the several designs which I was privileged to submit, preference was given to the one now being realized...the matter should therefore not be referred to myself; my duty is to preserve most scrupulously that which I have had orders to preserve..."

The proceedings which took several months ended with the conclusion that it was impossible to carry out the rebuilding of St Isaac's Cathedral "according to the designs of the architect Montferrand".

The committee members decided that building work could not be resumed before the existing designs had been corrected. President of the Academy of Arts Olenin reported this to Alexander I, and the emperor proposed that the committee should make the necessary corrections, always bearing in mind that Montferrand's principal postulates (five domes and columned porticoes) should be retained. Questions pertaining to the Cathedral's interior space, main dome and lighting were left to the committee's discretion. All individual proposals for the improvement of the design or for any new design were to comply with the demand "to preserve, wherever possible, the existing walls, but especially the old and new foundations". Montferrand was permitted to take part in the revision of the design on common grounds.

The architect was greatly upset by this setback, but he continued to work with remarkable persistence. He took into account the advice and criticism of the well-known Russian architects, benefited by the technological proposals of engineers, and was soon able to produce a new version of the design which was considerably better and technically more safe than the initial project.

The new design of the Cathedral envisaged four porticoes instead of two. The central part of the building was to be emphasized by a square area formed by four piers supporting the main dome. This construction would eliminate the danger of sagging. According to the revised design, which gained the approval of the emperor, only a very small portion of the old edifice was to be preserved: the walls of the sanctuary, the foundation and the two piers on the eastern side. The façades received a totally new treatment: Montferrand decided in favour of a pyramidal solution.

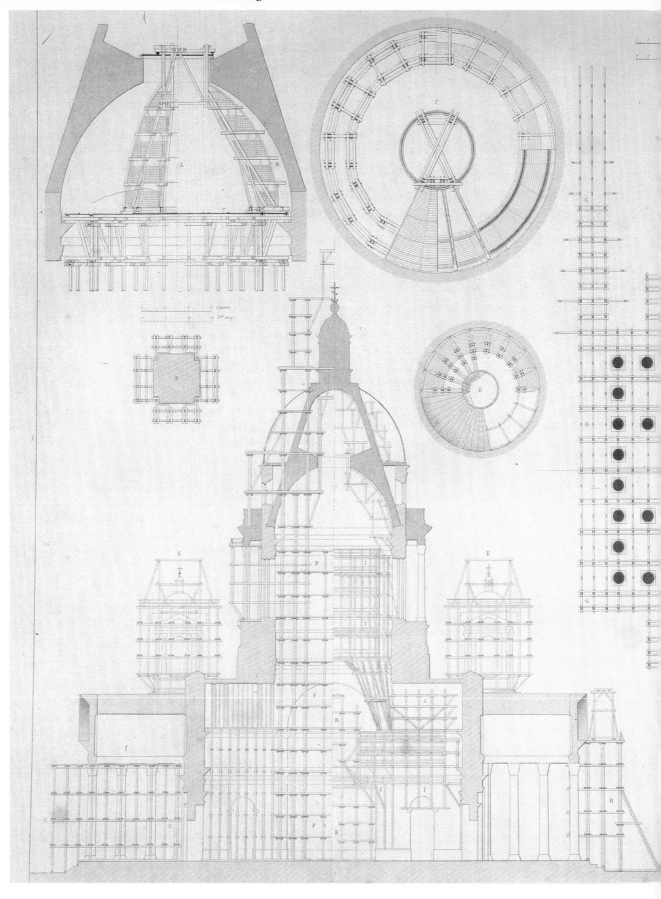

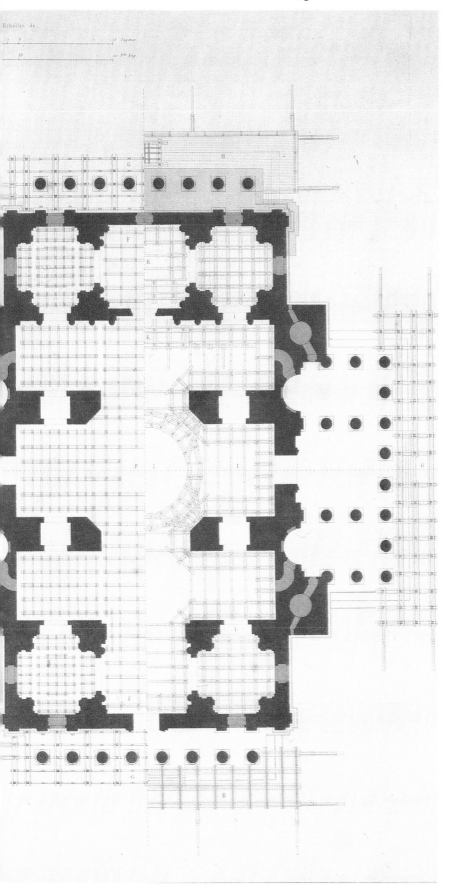

Plan and Cross-section of Scaffolds Raised on the Construction Site of St Isaac's Cathedral. Lithograph after a drawing by Auguste Montferrand. 1845

Longitudinal Section of St Isaac's Cathedral According to the 1825 Design. Lithograph after a drawing by Auguste Montferrand. 1845

Montferrand's revised design received official approval on 3 April 1825. A new stage in the construction of St Isaac's Cathedral began.

Both Alexander I, and Nicholas I who succeeded him, followed closely the progress of the construction work. The emperor and the Holy Synod carefully examined some of the elements of the design and exercised control over the decoration of the Cathedral. Nicholas I was the top moderator in all matters: he chose the subjects for the paintings and sculptures of the exterior and interior. On countless occasions he interfered with the progress of the work. His instructions were far from always being in harmony with the artistic visions of the Cathedral's architect and of the artists and sculptors who worked on its decoration.

The Commission for the Construction of St Isaac's Cathedral, which had been approved by Alexander I in 1818, also took charge of the works. It included top-ranking officials: the chairman was Count Nikolai Golovin, member of the State Council; among its founding members were Osip Kozodavlev, Minister of Home Affairs, and Count Alexander Golitsyn, Minister of Public Education. The appointment to the Commission of men of such calibre indicated the importance attached to the project by the emperor.

The four decades which it took to build St Icaac's, 1818 to 1858, spanned a whole epoch in the development of Russian architecture and building techniques. Architectural and structural problems were solved with the participation of renowned architects and esteemed scientists and engineers of the age: Augustin Béthencourt, Karl Oppermann, Léon Carbonier, Peter Lomnovsky, Pierre Clapeyron, Gabriel Lamé, and others.

The beginning of the construction work coincided with the flowering of Classicism. By the middle of the nineteenth century, however, its gradual decline was marked by a loss of stylistic purity, a departure from the principle of architectural and decorative unity, and a tendency to indulge in ornamental elements which had no structural meaning. These features heralded the beginning of Eclecticism in architecture. St Isaac's Cathedral, the last major building in Russia designed in the classic style, already shows certain influence of this new trend. Naturally, this added to the complexity of the task that confronted Montferrand.

The Building:
A Record of Its Construction

After the founding ceremony of St Isaac's Cathedral in June 1819, work on the building's foundations was started. Montferrand was faced with the complex task of linking the old footing to the new.

In St Petersburg the larger buildings all had pile-supported foundations. To build them, deep trenches were dug and the ground water pumped out. After that piles of pine, over six metres long and 26 to 28 centimetres in diameter, were treated with tar and driven into the earth. The intervals between the piles were equal to their diameter.

Cast-iron drivers were used to do the work. Windlasses drawn by six horses raised the pile-drivers. The piles were sunk into the ground with measured thrusts until the ground between them was packed so hard that a pointed iron bar would enter it only with great effort. After that ten test strikes were made. If the pile would not go deeper, it was cut off with the supervisor's authorization. Montferrand reported to the Commission that in the month of August five piles were installed daily, but in November the number dropped to two. As a result the pile-driving stage took up a whole year.

For uniform cutting of the piles Montferrand employed an old and popular method. The pumps that removed the ground water were stopped; when the water reached the preset level, it was again pumped out, and the piles could then be trimmed according to the mark left by the water. The spaces between the piles were filled with pressed charcoal to the depth of one metre. It took a total of 10,762 piles to accomplish the necessary work.

Most of the large buildings in St Petersburg rested on strip footings, but Montferrand wanted a net foundation for St Isaac's because that would ensure a better connection with the old footing and would prevent the massive edifice from sagging.

Work on the Cathedral's foundation, supervised by Montferrand and a stone-masonry expert, went on for nearly five years. It took an army of 125,000 workers: stone-masons, carpenters and forgers.

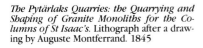

The Pytärlaks Quarries: the Quarrying and Shaping of Granite Monoliths for the Columns of St Isaac's. Lithograph after a drawing by Auguste Montferrand. 1845

The monolithic granite blocks needed for the columns were obtained from the Pytärlaks quarries in Finland, not far from Vyborg. For more than thirty years the Pytärlaks quarries had provided granite for St Petersburg and other Russian cities. The site was chosen because it had several advantages, such as its proximity to the deep-fairway bay and the post road, which ensured a regular supply of manpower, tools and foodstuffs.

Despite the harsh climate with low temperatures and snowstorms and the damp sea air, work at Pytärlaks went on the year round. After a visit to the quarry Montferrand made the following entry in his diary:

"Great as our surprise was when the granite rocks came into view, it gave way to still greater admiration as we beheld in the first quarry the seven columns that had not yet been worked up..."

During his visits to Pytärlaks Montferrand was strongly impressed by the physical strength and practical skill of the Russian workers and their well coordinated teamwork. "The mining of granite," wrote Montferrand, "an occupation that is not too common elsewhere, is widespread in Russia where they handle it quite well... craftsmanship that amazes us is regarded here as an everyday pursuit and surprises no one."

The mining of granite for St Isaac's columns was supervised by a contractor from Vologda Province whose name was Samson Sukhanov.

Starting in 1819 Russian newspapers regularly carried materials on the progress of the works, and printed information about contractual opportunities. Thus, in 1819 *Sankt-Peterburgskiye Vedomosti* (St Petersburg Gazette) carried the following notice: "The Commission for the Construction of St Isaac's Cathedral requests persons wishing to undertake the building of flat-bottomed boats for the transportation of granite." This contract went to the large-scale industrialist Charles Berd. He had the necessary boats built at one of his factories with surprising speed.

The granite monoliths for St Isaac's columns were rolled down to the shore and loaded on a barge which was towed by two steam tugs across the Gulf of Finland to the landing-stage on the Neva. After the unloading the monoliths were taken to the construction site where they were worked up and polished.

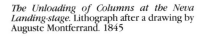

The Unloading of Columns at the Neva Landing-stage. Lithograph after a drawing by Auguste Montferrand. 1845

The unloading of the huge columns for the porticoes was a most impressive sight. "The public found it hard to imagine how the transportation could be effected: even if a means of raising these huge blocks from the ground could be found, would it be humanly possible to carry them over so a large distance? For many days the public anticipated this event," wrote Dupré de Saint-Maure, the French traveller who happened to be in St Petersburg at the time. He continued: "An immense crowd occupied the embankment and St Isaac's Square in order to witness the wonder... This is an ideal display of human patience, strength and skill."

Another account was left us by Nokolai Bestuzhev, a gifted journalist and painter, who was later to take part in the uprising of 14 December 1825. In one of his essays he rebuked the editors of Russian newspapers and magazines for failing to take proper notice of this truly popular feat. This is what he wrote: "We search for wonders in strange lands; we avidly peruse ancient histories recording the titanic feats of architecture in olden times, and exclaim at every line: unbelievable!... And we pass by these marvellous, unbelievable columns with no more than mere curiosity. The huge size of these columns, the simple methods which Nature herself has taught to our common folk... all this fills my heart with a pleasant feeling which seems to tell me that I, a Russian, have outgrown foreigners by a full inch."

The Installation of the North Portico Columns. Lithograph after a drawing by Auguste Montferrand. 1845

The Hauling of Marble Blocks. Lithograph after a drawing by Auguste Montferrand. 1845

When the time came at last for the columns to be raised onto their bases, all the eye-witnesses of the event were filled with wonder and admiration. The installation of the first column was attended by the imperial family, by foreign guests and architects who came to St Petersburg to see the ceremony. The Cathedral square and the roofs of the nearby houses were packed with spectators.

To raise the columns and install them in the porticoes, special high scaffolds had to be built, with three clear spans between four rows of vertical poles that were covered by cross-beams. Placed alongside were sixteen cast-iron capstans. Each column, covered with felt and matting, was secured with strong ropes and rolled into one of the spans between the poles. The ropes' ends were attached to the capstans by a system of pulleys. Each capstan was driven by eight workers. It took less than an hour to install a column. Montferrand noted proudly that "the wooden construction of the scaffolds ... was perfect to such an extent that not a single creak was heard during all the fourty-eight installations". Everything had been verified and calculated with the greatest accuracy, for the slightest error could have halted all work on the site and cause damage on a disastrous scale.

The Cathedral has sixteen columns in the south and north porticoes each, with eight columns on the east and the west sides. Each column of one solid block of granite weighs 114 tons and is 17 metres high; its diameter is 1.8 metres. The first of the 48 columns was installed on 20 March 1828; the last, on 11 August 1830.

All in all, St Isaac's decorative ensemble comprises 112 monolithic columns of different sizes.

Building the porticoes before raising the outer walls obviously ran counter to architectural principles, but Montferrand had to do this because of the formidable task presented by the installation of the grandiose columns.

The Cathedral has outer walls of brick 2.5 to 5 metres thick. Together with the marble facing, they are four times as thick as the walls of most civil buildings.

The mortar needed for the walls and the piers supporting the dome was prepared with particular care. Lime and sand were sieved into vats to form alternating layers. The compound was kept in the vats for three days and nights before it was applied.

The marble lining (5 or 6 centimetres thick on the outside walls, and 1 or 1.5 centimetres thick in the interior) was attached to the wall surfaces by means of metal staples at the same time that the walls were raised.

Iron braces of different contours were incorporated in the brickwork to assure greater safety. The metal bindings were hand-forged. The forgers also manufactured the metal rafters for the roof, elements for the construction of the dome and other details.

In 1836, the walls and piers were finally ready. Work was started on the roofings. In addition to the brick vaults, interior decorative vaults were built. Their iron frame was covered with a metal grid and faced with scagliola (imitation marble). The interior vaults have a purely decorative function.

By 1837 the base of the drum was constructed, and this enabled the builders to begin the installation of the upper colonnade, consisting of 24 columns. They were placed on special trolleys and taken up over a planked ramp.

Many innovations were applied on the construction site. For example, a special device consisting of two cast-iron discs was used to turn the columns in the required direction; inserted in the grooves of the lower disc were metal balls (an anticipation of the ball-bearing principle). St Isaac's was Russia's first construction site to be fitted with a rail track to transport the huge blocks of granite.

The Hoisting Up of a Column for the Drum of the Dome. Lithograph after a drawing by Auguste Montferrand. 1845

Montferrand proposed that metal structures should be used to build the main dome instead of brickwork. The dome was to have an outer facing of copper. In his own words, "the upper part of the Cathedral will be built entirely with cast-iron and iron..., and the dome itself will be sheathed with gilt copper".

To back up his decision Montferrand cited economic, technological and aesthetic arguments that were quite convincing. He pointed out that if the dome were built in this way, its cost "would be cut by two million and it would take only three years to build instead of six".

It was Montferrand's design that was implemented.

Archive materials show that the building of the main dome proceeded entirely by the testing method. The engineer Lomnovsky merely estimated the weight of the cast-iron structure instead of making the basic calculations. Credit for the constructional design of the metal dome undoubtedly goes to Montferrand. He made clever use of the idea of Christopher Wrenn, the architect of St Paul's Cathedral in London, choosing a system of conic and spheric vaults. Wrenn, however, had used brick as his main material. Montferrand acquitted himself with the honour of building an impressive metal dome which was also graceful and lightweight.

Metal Frame of the Main Dome. Lithograph after a drawing by Auguste Montferrand. 1845

490 tons of iron, 990 tons of cast-iron, 49 tons of copper and 30 tons of bronze went into the construction of the main dome. The metal structures and details were supplied by Berd's factory.

The main dome of St Isaac's comprises three connected structural parts. The inner part has a spheric shape, the middle is conic, and the outer is parabolic. The outer dome's diameter is 25.8 metres. 100,000 hollow clay pots of conic shape, resonators, were inserted between the girders. The use of resonators dates back to the early Roman structures; they were also employed in the building of Russian churches. Cemented with mortar, the pots made the dome less heavy, provided a fine heat-isolating band and ensured better acoustics.

The inner (spherical) dome was planked with wooden boards that were coated with tar-treated felt. It was then covered with plaster and decorated with murals. The middle, conic dome was given an interior coating of copper sheets painted a bluish shade. The large bronze rays and stars which decorate its surface produce the effect of a starry sky, setting off the silver dove as the incarnation of the Holy Spirit.

On the outside the dome is faced with closely fitted copper gilt sheets.

It took years (from 1835 to 1843) to fire-gild the surface of the Cathedral's main dome, minor domes and crosses. Copper sheets were coated with a fluid compound of gold and mercury; the mercury was vaporized by slowly heating the copper sheets over braziers. The gilding process was repeated three times. Each sheet was stamped with the hallmark of the master responsible for the gilding standards.

It is customary for the Russian churches to have gilded tops, but the size of St Isaac's main dome gives it a unique status both in Russia and in Europe.

St Isaac's was by far the most impressive construction site in St Petersburg. The newspaper *Severnaya Pchela* (Northern Bee) had this to say about it: "In spite of all the buildings that rise every year to adorn St Petersburg, our public continues to take a special interest in the construction of the majestic church dedicated to St Isaac, which will be on a par with the greatest edifices of Europe ... Its appearance is impressive to such a degree that we form a mental picture of the colossal pyramidal structures that were the pride of ancient Egypt."

Visitors personally authorized by Montferrand were allowed to make a round of the construction site. They all believed the rising structure to be quite extraordinary.

In the course of fourty years the grandiose project drew into its vortex, at one time or another, over 400,000 workmen. Carpenters came from Kostroma, and stone-masons from the Arkhangelsk, Olonets and Vologda provinces. Thousands of skilled craftsmen from every part of Russia flocked to St Petersburg in search of a living.

Workmen were hired by contractors who had been authorized by the Commission for the Construction of St Isaac's Cathedral to act on its behalf. A contractor received a fixed sum for every workman recruited: a carpenter fetched him 50 roubles, and a worker engaged in pile-driving, 40 roubles. Every workman was regarded as the chattel of the contractor or the Commission. Those who deserted from the construction site were returned by force. The conditions on which the workers were hired were very harsh. Here is an excerpt from the contract between Tychinkin and Gerchin, two St Petersburg contractors, and the Commission: "The stone-masons and forgers engaged by us will work every day, including feast days but excluding Sundays, from morning till evening, as long as it is practicable in a given season." The workday lasted from dawn to dusk. It was shorter in autumn, but in summer it could be greatly stretched out because of the white nights of St Petersburg.

Under-age labourers were also employed on the construction site. The Commission's officer Borushkevich pointed out in one of his reports that the contractor Sukhanov employed boys whose physique and age were incompatible with the hard work assigned to them.

The workmen were undernourished and always in need of clothes and footwear. The worst off were the miners in the quarries run by Shikhin and Sukhanov.

Housing conditions were equally appalling. Next to the construction site stood barracks with earthen floors and bunks arranged in three tiers. In 1828, the Commission's executor Yevdakov reported that "overcrowding in the barracks caused extreme dampness, which provokes sickness...water drips from the walls, windows and ceilings...The window frames are dislocated, the floors have rotted away with the damp, and the stoves are out of order due to excessive use."

Accidents were frequent, especially when workers fell down from the high scaffolds; in the quarries hand and arm injuries were common. *Severnaya Pchela* had this to say on the matter: "The patience and firmness of these people must truly be extraordinary if they are able to endure their hard and monotonous labour."

The most dangerous occupation was the fire-gilding of the domes. Though it was carried out in the open, the workers were affected by the mercury vapours. The gilding caused the loss of several dozens lives: slowly but surely the mercury poisoning took effect.

Montferrand, who for many years had watched the Russian workmen, gave them a very high rating: "Russian workers are honest, courageous and patient. Endowed with exceptional intelligence...they stand out also for their kindly and open-hearted nature which is most appealing...They are possessed of a natural courage which makes them particularly fond of dangerous work. Clever craftsmen, they often prove to be real masters...they carry out the most complex and difficult jobs with surprising accuracy."

More than 130 years passed since the completion of the construction work, but even today the reliability of St Isaac's walls and vaults, the elaborate finish of its stone details, stucco mouldings and ormolu decorations testify to the craftsmanship of the Russians.

The Decorative Ensemble
Exterior Decoration

The majestic edifice of St Isaac's Cathedral is a dominant feature of two squares in the centre of Leningrad: St Isaac's Square and Decembrists' (formerly Senate) Square. Its gilded dome punctuates the city's skyline as confidently as the tall spire of the Sts Peter and Paul Cathedral and the famous "needle" of the Admiralty building.

St Isaac's is a compact volume, with each of its four façades flanked by grandiose Corinthian porticoes. The flat surfaces of the wall are broken up by arched windows with massive surrounds, and the four corners of the main block are ornamented with pilasters. The Cathedral is surmounted by four turrets serving as bell-towers, and an impressive dome with a complicated design: its tall drum is surrounded by a colonnade and crowned by a gilt top with an octagonal lantern.

Surround: something (as a decorative border or edging) around a window opening
Pilaster: an upright architectural member that is rectangular in plan, which projects from the wall and is architecturally treated as a column (with capital, shaft and base)

View of the south façade
▶

25

Angels with a Torch.
Sculptural group in
the attic's corner.
By Ivan Vitali.
1850-55

Drum and cupola
crowned with an
octagonal lantern

30

The statues and reliefs which adorn the building form a remark-
ably large (for the mid-nineteenth century) body of sculpture. The
works on the drum's balustrade, the cornices, the pediments and
outer doors were done by the eminent sculptors Ivan Vitali and Piotr
Klodt, and also by Joseph Hermann, François Lemaire and Alexander
Loganovsky.

The distribution of the sculptures corresponds to the basic
division of the building. They unite the architectural masses and
heighten the expressiveness of individual elements. The groups of
angels with torches, the work of Vitali, serve to link the basic volume
of the Cathedral to the crowning drum and dome. Hermann's statues
of angels emphasize the elegant form of the drum and harmonize with
the rhythmic articulation of the dome.

There are four large high reliefs in the tympana of the pediments.
The relief of the south portico depicts The *Adoration of the Magi*
while the western relief presents *St Isaac Blessing the Emperor
Theodosius* (both are by Vitali). The sculptor added to the main
characters, who are treated conventionally, several realistic figures
representing his own contemporaries. We know that he made the
heads of the Ethiopian king and his page, an Ethiopian boy, from life:
Ethiopian servants of the staff of the imperial household posed for him.
In the noblemen of the Emperor's entourage, Victor and Saturnius, we
recognize Prince Piotr Volkonsky, Chairman of the Commission for
the Construction of St Isaac's, and Alexei Olenin, President of the
Academy of Arts. Montferrand, wearing a toga, reclines in a corner of
this pediment, holding a model of St Isaac's.

The north pediment has a high relief of *The Resurrection* while the
east pediment depicts The *Meeting Between St Isaac and the Emperor
Valens.* Both reliefs are by Lemaire.

Figures of the Apostles and the Evangelists decorate the cornices
and corners of the pediments.

Interior Decoration

Work on the Cathedral's interior decoration began in 1841.
Before Montferrand's design received final approval, the architect had
had to endure a severe blow.

Nicholas I took it into his head to entrust the design of the
Cathedral's interior to Leo von Klenze, the architect who came to
work in Russia in 1839. It took the latter two years to produce his
project. Paradoxially enough, instead of designing the decor to fit the
existing building, he wanted the building to be fitted to his own plan.
This would necessitate making apertures in the vaults to admit more
light, to destroy some of the cornices and to close some niches. Klenze
suggested that part of the painting work be entrusted to the German
artist Schrandorf and done by the encaustic method on copper gilt
plates.

The stucco mouldings and sculptures proposed by Klenze were
fragmentary and multifarious. When his design was submitted to the
Commission for the Construction of St Isaac's Cathedral, Montferrand
objected to the idea of tearing down parts of the finished building. He

Marble bust of Auguste Montferrand. By
Anton Foletti. 1857

pointed out that the design was at variance with the principles of the
Cathedral's interior decoration which had been formulated as
"splendour, nobility and opulence". He thereupon offered his own
design, and requested that a special commission be set up to examine
both projects so as to ward off all suspicions of bias against his rival.
The commission included Vasily Stasov, Konstantin Thon, Alexander
Briullov and Karl Rossi.

Montferrand's design earned unreserved approval. The commission pointed out that Klenze's scheme contained a large number of
unacceptable propositions that would detract from the Cathedral's
monumental aspect.

Thus began the concluding stage of the work, which was also a
new stage in Montferrand's life.

In the final version of the design for the Cathedral's interior
decoration, which was evolved by Montferrand in 1842, the arrangement of sculptures in the main dome followed the Classic pattern, the
decoration of the vaults was in the Baroque style, and the inner doors
showed the influence of the Italian Renaissance.

33

St Isaac's nave and the main iconostasis
◄

Capital: the head or crowning feature of a column or pilaster
Meander: an ornamental work or pattern consisting of small straight bars intersecting one another at right or oblique angles
Holy Doors: the central doors in the iconostasis of an Eastern Orthodox church
Iconostasis: partition with doors and (since the 15th century) tiers of icons that separates the sanctuary from the nave in an Eastern Orthodox church
Chapel: an additional place of worship in an Eastern Orthodox church with its own sanctuary

Detail of decoration of the main iconostasis: malachite roundel on coloured marble

The Cathedral interior impresses the viewer by its monumentality. The abundance of paintings, mosaics and sculptures, coupled with the semiprecious stones and gilt work, produces a rich variety of colour effects.

The general feeling is that the Cathedral's interior is overdecorated. The magnificent gilt capitals and elaborately figured bases on the columns and pilasters, the balustrades, the openwork railings with intricate designs incorporating the meander and winding plant motifs, the many-tiered decor of the arched vaults and passages, the gilt ornaments and fanciful details of the Holy Doors of the iconostases - all this can be hardly said to form a unity. But on closer inspection one is fascinated by the perfect design and execution of all the details.

400 kilograms of gold and 1,000 tons of bronze went into the decoration of the Cathedral. 16,000 kilograms of malachite and more than eleven square metres of lazurite from Badakhshan were used in the facing of the columns and architectural details of the high altar and two chapel altars. The floors, walls and piers are lined with the semiprecious Shoksha porphyry from the shores of Lake Onega, with black slate from the Caucasus and different marbles: the pink Tivdiya marble, the grey marble from Finland, the white Italian marble, the green marble of Genoa, the yellow marble of Siena, and red marble from France. Academician Alexander Fersman, the eminent Soviet mineralogist, described St Isaac's as a treasury of coloured stones equal to the Hermitage.

The facing of natural marble on the walls reaches up to the great cornice. The attic's facing is of scagliola.

The walls are covered with light-coloured Italian marble. The marble frames of the paintings placed in the niches stand out for the elegance and intricacy of the carving. The panels, roundels and meanders are of Italian marbles (Sienese yellow, Genoese green) and red *griotto* with darker veins, from the south of France. Decorative stones from various parts of the Russian Empire were also extensively used in the Cathedral's interior, e.g. grey marble that came from the environs of Vyborg was used to line the floor.

Attic: a low storey or wall above the main order of a building
Panel: a usually sunken section of a surface (as a wall, pier or door) set off by a moulding or other margin

West part of the nave

View of the main
iconostasis from the
nave
▶

The main iconostasis in side view
◄

The frieze that borders the piers and walls at the floor level, as well as the frieze of the great cornice that runs along the entire perimeter above the pilasters, are of Shoksha porphyry. This very hard stone of rare beauty is extremely difficult to work; after polishing it acquires a fine shade of very deep red.

The socle is faced with black slate that sets off to perfection the light-coloured marble of the walls. The pink Tivdiya marble graces the pilasters and piers.

The decoration of the altars is of special interest because of the striking unity attained in the combined employment of painting, mosaic and sculpture.

The iconostasis of the high altar is faced with white marble and adorned with ten pillars of malachite and two of lazurite; these pillars are one of the Cathedral's main treasures. The rich greens and blues of the pillars forcefully attract the visitor's eye.

Fersman described malachite as "a bright and buoyant stone", one of the finest minerals ever produced by nature. Its palette ranges from turquoise-green to deep shades of dark green. Malachite owes its name to the Greek word *molochites* meaning 'mallow', because the colour range of malachite resembles the green colour of this plant.

In Ancient Greece malachite was used to adorn state rooms. Malachite mined in the Sinai Peninsula was used in Ancient Egypt to make amulets, ear-rings, cameos and finger-rings of peerless beauty.

In Russia malachite was originally discovered in the foothills of the Urals in 1637, but it gained popularity and large-scale employment only in the late eighteenth and early nineteenth century, when two Urals mines began to yield over 80 tons of high-quality malachite in a wide range of greens annually. In 1835, a 250-ton malachite block was found in the Urals. Malachite then began to be employed both in jewellery-making and interior decoration. Fersman speaks of "the malachite period" in the history of Russian stone-cutting art. The mineral was mined in irregularly shaped massive blocks with impregnations of other minerals. It was the stone-cutter's task to fashion an *objet d'art* with a minimum amount of malachite. This was achieved with the help of the so-called "Russian mosaic" method: a base of stone or copper was covered with a mixture of beeswax and rosin, in which pieces of malachite were bedded. Then the surface was burnished perfectly smooth. This method was employed to produce the famous Malachite Room in St Petersburg Hermitage and the unique malachite pillars of St Isaac's Cathedral.

The pillars of the main iconostasis seem to be monolithic, but they are bronze cylinders covered with malachite pieces that are exquisitely matched for pattern and shade.

The pillars' patterns beautifully harmonize with the clear and logical decorative motif of the malachite insets in the lower borders of the iconostases. These insets are a rich display of different kinds of malachite.

The pillars, insets and roundels of St Isaac's taken as a whole are considered the largest malachite composition ever to be accomplished.

Equally valuable are the pillars and insets of lazurite.

Lazurite was renowned in antiquity for its bright blue colour. In the first century

View of the iconostasis in St Catherine's Chapel from the right-side arch of the main iconostasis

43

B.C. it was identified with sapphire; its later names, lapis lazuli and lazurite, originated in the eighteenth century.

In Ancient Egypt, Central Asia, Mesopotamia and China, in classical Greece and Rome, as well as in early Russia, lazurite was used to make jewellery. It is one of the costliest semiprecious stones. Its main deposits lie in north-east Afghanistan, and it had to be imported to Russia. Later lazurite was discovered in Siberia near Lake Baikal.

The two central pillars of the iconostasis, which were faced with Badakhshan lazurite cut at the Peterhof Lapidary Works, afford one of the few examples of the use of top-quality lazurite to produce monumental decorative works.

The two lazurite pillars of deep blue are at their best when the iconostasis is lit by the slanting rays of the evening sun, which cause the stone to glow with a beautiful shade of blue.

Arch: a typically curved structural member spanning an opening between two supports

The side arches that break up the surface of the main iconostasis afford a view of the Cathedral's two minor iconostases. These are of white Italian marble, with panels of malachite and other decorative stones, and their workmanship is in no way inferior to that of the main iconostasis. The greyish-pink marble facing in the east part of the chapels, which belonged to the church started by Rinaldi, is remarkable for the subtle beauty of its muted colours. It sets off to great advantage the white marble of the iconostases and the walls that separate the chapels from the main sanctuary.

The icons of the first and second tiers of the main iconostasis are in mosaic, while those of the third tier are oil paintings. The first-tier icons, executed after the paintings of Timoleon Karl von Neff, depict the name saints of the Russian monarchs during whose reign the four St Isaac's churches were built. The second-tier mosaics, executed after the paintings of Fiodor Briullov, are dedicated to the name saints of the imperial family. The painted icons of the third tier, which are the work of Semion Zhivago, represent the Old Testament prophets.

The general arrangement of painted decorations and a list of their subjects were drawn up by Montferrand in accordance with the instructions of the Holy Synod.

Sketches for the murals and pictures were examined by Montferrand, the Synod, the Council of the Academy of Arts, and the emperor. A finished painting was examined by the Synod, and it was only after its approval that the artist was entitled to receive his fee.

Karl Briullov recalled the following incident: "One day, when I came home at a very late hour, I discovered on my desk a paper from the Court Minister with orders to present myself at the Anichkov Palace the following morning. There I found Bruni, Basin, and von Neff. The Emperor took us to his study, showed us Guercino's head of Christ, praising it to the skies, saying that he never saw a better one … and wished that the Russian artists took it for a type." In this way the Christ by Guercino, a Baroque Italian artist, was set up as the model for all the paintings in St Isaac's Cathedral.

The quality of the murals' execution depended largely on the quality of the priming. The plaster surface was trimmed with pumice stone, heated up to 100—200 °C with braziers or preheated cast-iron plates, and covered with a paste of beeswax, oil and powdered lead. Several layers of this paste were applied on the wall's surface. A layer of white lead was applied over it.

The priming often proved deficient, and had to be done over several times. In

1855, satisfactory results were at last obtained, and by 1858 the painting work had been mostly accomplished.

The Cathedral possesses a collection of murals and paintings in oils done in the mid-nineteenth century that is the only one of its kind in Russia. The paintings in its west part present Old Testament subjects, and those in the east part are dedicated to themes from the Gospels.

The creation of such a large cycle of icons and murals quite naturally became a major event in the artistic life of Russia.

No official competition was held. Paintings were commissioned from artists mostly on the basis of the personal likes and dislikes of the emperor and the high-placed Synod officials. Yet the list of contributors includes the names of outstanding painters who were the finest exponents of the Russian Classical school: Vasily Shebuyev, Fiodor Bruni, Karl Briullov, Nikolai Alexeyev and Piotr Basin, and this speaks for itself.

Among those who were entrusted with the painting work were also some less distinguished artists, like Alexei Markov and Franz Riss. For them work in the Cathedral was a welcome opportunity to improve their skill.

Of special importance for the younger artists was the fact that all the painting work done in the Cathedral was supervised by Vasily Shebuyev, a painter who enjoyed wide renown.

A prominent exponent of the nineteenth-century academic school in Russia, Shebuyev had given instruction at the Academy of Arts for many years before he became its president. He earned special recognition for his murals on the dome of the Academy's Council Hall. Among Shebuyev's best known pieces are *The Death of Hippolytus* and *A Merchant's Exploit.*

Shebuyev executed four paintings for St Isaac's Cathedral, of which the most successful is *The Raising of the Widow's Son of Nain.* The composition of the scene, the arrangement of the figures, the brilliant draughtsmanship — all warrants the unofficial title of "the grand professor" which Shebuyev earned in his lifetime. Members of the Academy Council were so impressed by this particular painting that they were moved to bare their heads when it was presented for their approval.

The painting of the vaults was entrusted in 1836 to Fiodor Bruni, one of the best-known Russian artists.

Bruni's outstanding talent had emerged at the early age of eleven. He was trained at the Academy of Arts where his teacher was Shebuyev. Bruni graduated with flying colours and left for Italy. His paintings *Death of Camilla, the Sister of the Horatii* and *The Bronze Serpent* were a success in Europe. Well-thought-out compositions, masterful draughtsmanship, and clever introduction of prominent civic ideas into religious subjects – these are the most attractive features of Bruni's masterpieces.

For St Isaac's interior Bruni produced 25 cartoons, which were highly appreciated by the public at exhibitions held in Rome and St Petersburg. Bruni and his pupils Karl Wenig, Pavel Pleshanov and Nikolai Ksenofontov executed twelve murals for the vaults and attic.

Taking into account the poor lighting of the vaults and their great height, Bruni opted for large-scale, strongly contoured figures and vivid colour patches that make every detail stand out clearly even in the dim light of the Cathedral.

Bruni's composition *The Flood* in the north part of the Cathedral goes beyond the framework of the Old Testament subject. It is a large-scale narrative with a profound psychological meaning. Depicting the reactions of a few people, Bruni was able to demonstrate a wide range of human experiences, weaknesses and wrong-doings. His characteristic blue-grey colouring adds to the general mood of tragic hopelessness.

A typical work of the Academic school, *The Flood* was expected by Synod officials to project the idea of justified divine punishment. Bruni's masterly handling of the subject, however, stimulates controversial thoughts and feelings. *The Flood* is undoubtedly one of the best murals in the Cathedral.

In the 1830s Fiodor Bruni was a recognized authority and the head of the Russian Classical school. He was the Keeper of the Hermitage Picture Gallery and head of the mosaic section at the Academy of Arts. After Shebuyev's death he succeeded him as the Academy's president.

Nave: the long central hall in a church; in a case of several naves they are separated by rows of pillars or columns

In the central part of the vaults Bruni painted *The Vision of the Prophet Ezekiel* and over the nave, *The Last Judgement,* a fine composition, which projects the idea of God's omnipotence and the smallness and shallowness of humans and their life. In the centre of this mural we see Christ and the Archangels. On a black cover at his feet is a skeleton and a broken scythe: symbols of overpowered Death; on the sides are the righteous and the sinners. In keeping with the instructions of Synod officials, the figure of Christ is painted in the tradition of early Russian icons.

The Cathedral's largest mural (its area is more than 800 square metres) appears on the ceiling of the main dome. The subject is *The Virgin in Majesty,* and the artist is Karl Briullov.

Briullov had painted many effective genre scenes and glittering formal portraits before he earned European renown with *The Last Day of Pompeii.* In 1842, he was commissioned to do some of St Isaac's paintings, and this gave him a chance to prove himself as a monumentalist. As he worked on countless preliminary drawings, Briullov experienced a surge of creative power and used to tell his pupils: "I need more space, I would like to paint upon the sky." He was strongly influenced by Michelangelo's murals and hoped to produce in St Isaac's an impressive ensemble that would be his true claim to fame. He worked long hours, never leaving the high scaffoldings.

Briullov's concentrated work in the unfinished damp building undermined his health. The marble dust, the sharp temperature changes due to the open windows of the drum of the dome provoked a rheumatic attack which caused a cardiac condition. Briullov had to ask leave to quit the job. He took the doctors' advice and went to Italy for a cure. He died in that country in 1852.

Briullov painted nearly all of the ceiling mural's main figures. The middle ground and the background were done by Piotr Basin, who also did the figures of the Apostles, the Evangelists and the Passion series following Briullov's cartoons and studies.

The Vision of the Prophet Ezekiel. Painting on a ceiling vault. By Fiodor Bruni. 1851-53

The Last Judgement. Painting on a ceiling vault. By Fiodor Bruni. 1849-53

The Creation of the Sun and the Moon. Painting on a ceiling vault. By Fiodor Bruni. 1846-53
►

View of the main
dome and its pen-
dentives
The Virgin in Majesty.
Ceiling painting
of the main dome.
By Karl Briullov
(with the assistance
of Piotr Basin).
1843-45

The Assumption.
Ceiling painting
of the minor dome
in St Catherine's
Chapel. By Piotr
Basin. 1846-49

The ceiling composition of the main dome, *The Virgin in Majesty,* depicts Mary surrounded by the saints. The essential requirement in painting murals is the ability to present the subject avoiding excessive details and using broad, free brushstrokes. *The Virgin in Majesty* proves that Briullov had a perfect command of this method.

The paintings that appear in the niches of the Cathedral's piers deserve special mention. The Synod decided to forego the traditional arrangement of icons dedicated to the Holy Week and icons of the Church Festival cycle. From the sixteenth century on these subjects had been traditionally placed in the third tier of the Russian iconostasis, but in St Isaac's they are mounted in the niches of the piers.

The entire cycle of 22 icons was done by Timoleon von Neff, Charles de Steuben and Cesare Mussini.

Neff was an acknowledged master of religious subjects. He contributed seven works for St Isaac's niches. A characteristic example of his style is *The Presentation of the Virgin.*

Steuben preferred episodes charged with dramatic tension. His style is best represented by *The Crucifixion,* executed along the strict lines of Academic painting.

Mussini, the author of popular scenes from the history of medieval Italy, contributed six works steeped in the traditions of the Italian Academic school. They stand out for their fine composition and impeccable execution.

The excessive humidity and low temperature in the Cathedral building soon made it imperative that painted compositions be replaced with mosaic pictures.

It is hardly feasible to give the precise date of the emergence of mosaic as an art. In classic Greece and Rome the term was used to describe the art of forming patterns or pictures by joining together small pieces of variously coloured glass, marble, or other material, which were held in place by a gum or pitch.

In the middle of the nineteenth century, the predominant technique of mosaic production in Europe was the Roman: pieces of coloured glass made in thin slabs – smalti – were attached to a hard surface. This method was ideally suited to the execution of mosaic copies of paintings because such copies ensured maximum fidelity.

Smalt, a pigment prepared by fusing glass and metallic oxides, can be made in a wide range of colours. Auros oxides yield shades of pink and purple, copper oxides produce reds and greens, and blue shades are obtained with cobalt.

Mosaic has the advantage of being durable. Giorgio Vasari, the renowned art historian of the Renaissance, noted that in contrast to painting which quickly deteriorated and disappeared, mosaics could be defined as "eternal pictures".

In Russia the earliest mention of mosaic occurs in the eleventh century in connection with the building of the Cathedral of St Sophia in Kiev. Due to a number of economic and political reasons this art later fell into decay.

In the eighteenth century, the famous Russian scholar Mikhail Lomonosov took an interest in the art of mosaic. He thoroughly studied this technique and the methods of the production of smalto, and founded a mosaic workshop. Lomonosov and his pupils produced several mosaic compositions, including the well-known *Battle of Poltava.* After Lomonosov's death this art fell into disuse for almost a hundred years.

*The Presentation of
the Virgin.* Painting
in the niche of
a pier. By Timoleon
von Neff. 1846-48

*The Nativity of the
Virgin.* Painting in
the niche of a pier.
By Timoleon von
Neff. 1846-48

St Catherine. Mosaic icon in the second tier of the iconostasis of St Catherine's Chapel. After a painting by Timoleon von Neff. 1868-80

The idea of replacing paintings with mosaic pictures must have come to Montferrand when he became fully aware of one of the Cathedral building's irreparable deficiencies: the impossibility of ensuring in it the temperature and humidity levels needed for the preservation of oil painting.

During his tour of Europe in 1843 Montferrand visited Italy. There he explored the possibilities of introducing mosaics into St Isaac's interior.

Irrespective of Montferrand's plans, the Academy of Arts was at that time examining the project of launching a mosaic workshop in St Petersburg. The scheme was first proposed by Krivtsov, who was in charge of the Russian artists based in Rome, and by Academician Georg Weckler.

During his visit to Italy in 1846 Nicholas I saw some mosaic icons in a Roman cathedral. He thereupon made up his mind about replacing St Isaac's paintings with mosaic compositions.

The artists Vasily Rayev, Yegor Solntsev, Ivan Shapovalov and Stepan Fiodorov, graduates of the Academy of Arts, then on their Academy-sponsored Roman tour, were directed to stay in Rome for an additional term in order to train in the art of mosaic under Michelangelo Barberi. Several years later a Russian mosaic workshop was established in Rome, with the artists Filippo Cocchi and Rubicondi training Russian mosaicists.

In response to a report by the Academy's president, the emperor gave orders (on 8 July 1847) that outlays on the upkeep of the mosaic workshop in Rome would be defrayed by the State Treasury.

In 1851, the workshop with its staff of Russian mosaicists and their Italian instructors was moved to St Petersburg.

In addition to Cocchi and Rubicondi, two specialists in chemistry were engaged (the brothers Justiano and Leopoldo Bonafede). When Cocchi and Rubicondi left for Italy in 1856, Justiano Bonafede was appointed the chief chemical expert. Later he was put in charge of both the technical and artistic matters. The departed Italians were replaced by Russian mosaicists Alexeyev, Khmelevsky, Lebedev, and others.

After a course of training in Italy, the artists brought to Russia several works executed by them: *St Nicholas,* a copy of the mosaic floor in Otricoli in the environs of Terni, and heads of the four Evangelists. These works are at present deposited at the Hermitage. This was the preparatory stage for executing the mosaics of St Isaac's. The Academy's mosaic workshop was soon able to produce necessary smalti.

Russian smalto has an exceptionally rich colour range. In addition to smalti of the primary colours and half-tints, pieces of a new kind were produced. They combined several shades of the same colour, or were multicoloured and with veins. They were extremely valuable because their application enabled mosaicists to make superior copies of oil paintings. Intricate painterly tasks could be resolved, and the originals' colouring could be reproduced with remarkable fidelity.

A very important component of the art of mosaic was the production of "golden smalti", which were used for the backgrounds of mosaic pictures. Molten glass was poured over gold leaves attached to glass plates; gold leaf and glass were fused under pressure. Smalti of this kind were widely used for the mosaics of St Isaac's Cathedral.

Mosaic work in the Cathedral was started in 1851 and finished in 1914. The first painting to be replaced by a mosaic copy was *The Saviour* from the main iconostasis. Later other mosaic copies were executed after the paintings of Neff, such as *St Catherine* (mosaicists Alexander Frolov, Landblat and Friedrich Hartung) and *St Nicholas of Myra* (mosaicists Shapovalov, Muravyov and Shchetinin).

These mosaic icons stand out for the subtle rendering of the play of light and shade and for the texture of different objects: the cold glint of metal, the sheen of the satin robes, and the living warmth of a human hand. In their efforts to reproduce exactly the rich palette of the oil paintings mosaicists had to employ smalti of more than 12,000 different shades.

Among the paintings and murals replaced by mosaic copies were those in the first and second tiers of the iconostases, and some compositions in the Cathedral's attic and pendentives: the Passion series and the four Evangelists.

Pendentive: one of the triangular sections of vaulting that is one of the means by which a circular dome or drum is supported over a square or polygonal compartment

The Last Supper. Mosaic icon in the third tier of the main iconostasis. After a painting by Semion Zhivago. 1879-87

The Last Supper, the central mosaic of the high altar (after the painting by Semion Zhivago), was executed in the technique of the optical mixture of colours: variously coloured smalti were chosen in such a way that at a distance their colours blended into the required tone. Judas' white cloak is an excellent example of this. On closer inspection we see that the smalti used here are of a great variety of shades – greenish, yellowish, bluish, and others.

The mosaics of later periods were made in a technique different from the one used in the iconostases. A case in point is *St Peter,* placed in the drum of the dome. The surface is left unpolished. The smalti, set at different angles and depths, form a sparkling, uneven surface, with light playing on their edges.

St Catherine. Mosaic icon in the first tier of the main iconostasis. After a painting by Timoleon von Neff. 1855-62

The Virgin and Child. Mosaic icon in the first tier of the main iconostasis. After a painting by Timoleon von Neff. 1854-56

St Nicholas of Myra. Mosaic icon in the first tier of the main iconostasis. After a painting by Timoleon von Neff. 1855-62

St John the Evangelist. Mosaic in a pendentive of the main dome. After a painting by Piotr Basin. 1873-84

Christ Bearing the Cross. Mosaic in the attic above a pilaster. After a painting by Piotr Basin. 1873-85

At the 1862 World Fair in London the mosaics of St Isaac's Cathedral were highly praised. Specialists agreed that the production of smalto at the Russian mosaic works had reached a degree of excellence unattained elsewhere in Europe.

Characteristically, the Cathedral's best-executed mosaics are the joint work of several masters. The expert supervision of Fiodor Bruni and Alexander Frolov greatly contributed to their excellence.

The stained-glass window in the depth of the sanctuary of St Isaac's depicts the Resurrection. It is probably the only stained-glass decoration to be found in an Eastern Orthodox Church.

The stained-glass art originated in the ninth century and became widespread in Italy, France and Germany, i.e. in the pre-eminently Catholic countries.

In Catholic churches stained glass was used for the windows. At first pieces of stained glass were mounted in a haphazard fashion to form a variously coloured surface. Later they began to be mounted in such a way as to produce figures. The art of stained-glass pictures had fully developed by the middle of the twelfth century. Later it reached an even higher peak of accomplishment.

To produce stained glass, glass coloured with metallic oxides was used, just as in the production of smalto.

The end of the sixteenth century marked the appearance of many-layered stained glass.

The introduction of lead frames made it possible to enlarge the size of stained-glass windows.

The stained-glass art reached its height in the thirteenth and fourteenth centuries. Towards the second half of the eighteenth century it experienced a decline, only to be revived in the first half of the nineteenth century. It was then that Master Frank won renown for his fine compositions. He was the head of special works set up in Munich at the Royal Porcelain Factory. His successor, Max Emmanuel Einmiller, improved the methods of the production of many-layered glass. He managed to make panels of two layers, both coloured, whilst previously one layer was always of clear class, and obtained more than 100 colours and shades of many-layered glass.

Stained-glass windows from the Royal Factory in Munich were considered to be the finest in Europe, and Einmiller was entrusted with making the stained-glass composition for St Isaac's Cathedral.

Montferrand suggested that stained glass should be used for the window in the sanctuary behind the main iconostasis when he worked on his first design of the Cathedral. He returned to this idea at a later stage and secured the whole-hearted approval of the emperor and the Commission.

The stained-glass window was commissioned in November 1841. Changes in the original sketch were made on several occasions. The final design was evolved by the German artist Heinrich Maria von Hess and the work was finished by the end of 1843. In the summer of 1844 crates containing parts of the stained-glass window were brought to St Petersburg by boat. Kühl, a master from the Munich Factory, assembled the window, and mounted it temporarily for a preview by Nicholas I. After that it was dismounted to await the conclusion of work in the east part of the Cathedral.

The stained-glass window consists of two iron frames (outer and inner) tied by metal rods. The outer frame is glazed with colourless glass. The stained glass is set

The Resurrection.
Stained-glass window in the main sanctuary. Made after a drawing by Heinrich Maria von Hess. 1841-43

Christ in Majesty.
Composition crowning the Holy Doors of the main iconostasis. Mosaic after a painting by Semion Zhivago; sculpture by Piotr Klodt; painting by Timoleon von Neff. 1850s-1860s
▶

65

The Resurrection. Sculptural group crowning the iconostasis in St Catherine's Chapel. By Nikolai Pimenov. 1850s

The Transfiguration. Sculptural group crowning the iconostasis in the Chapel of St Alexander Nevsky. By Nikolai Pimenov. 1850s

Bas-relief: sculptural relief in which the projection from the surrounding surface is less than half of the natural circumference

Galvanoplasty: the production of copies of medals, statues, reliefs, etc. by electrolysis; galvanoplasty was invented in 1838 by the Russian physicist and engineer Boris Yakobi

in the inner frame. The panels are held by metal strips attached to the frame on the front side. The small pieces of semi-transparent glass are held by lead calms. The window's total area is 28.5 square metres.

The sculptural decoration of St Isaac's interior includes figures of the Apostles, prophets and angels on the vaults and in the drum of the main dome, bas-reliefs in the iconostases and on the inner doors, and the ornamentation of the vaults. In the east part of the Cathedral are the attributes of the Eastern Orthodox church. The main sculptures are in ormolu, and those of the vaults are of copper (made with the galvanoplastic method).

The Holy Doors of the main iconostasis are crowned by the sculptural group *Christ in Majesty,* the work of Piotr Klodt.

The side aisles lead to the chapels where the iconostases are decorated with the sculptural groups of *The Resurrection* (the chapel of St Catherine) and *The Transfiguration* (the chapel of St Alexander Nevsky). Both groups, the work of Nikolai Pimenov, are in full harmony with the architectural forms of the chapels and create the overall impression of lightness and upward movement.

The Holy Doors
of the main icono-
stasis. Ormolu and
mosaic

The logical and compositional centre of *The Resurrection,* which includes five personages, is the figure of Christ, done in the Classic style. The angels have some features of the Baroque, which can be seen also in the figures of Roman soldiers in the lower tier.

The Transfiguration is conceived in a more emotional style.

The sculptures in the two chapels earned Pimenov the rank of professor in 1854; he was subsequently invited to teach at the Academy of Arts.

On the whole the chapels of St Catherine and St Alexander Newsky stand out for the colourful variety of their decorations, the costly materials used for them and the impeccable execution.

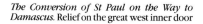
The Conversion of St Paul on the Way to Damascus. Relief on the great west inner door

The figures on the vaults of the drum were done by Ivan Vitali in 1845-50 with the active participation of two other sculptors, Zaleman and Beliayev. The ornaments were modelled by Dylev under Vitali's supervision, and moulded at the works of the Duke of Leichtenberg by the method of galvanoplasty.

The figures of prophets, patriarchs and angels, represented in complex and dynamic turns, are strongly foreshortened because they were intended to be viewed from below. They seem too large for their shallow niches.

Vitali also executed the reliefs on the three great inner doors (after drawings by Konstantin Moldavsky). The doors are divided into panels, and their composition recalls the Gate of Paradise by Lorenzo Ghiberti in the Baptistery of Florence. Their area is 42 square metres, and their weight, approximately 20 tons. The oakwood-and-bronze panels are decorated with many-figured reliefs. Those of the great north door present scenes from the life of St Isaac the Dalmatian and St Nicholas of Myra, while the south door carries scenes from early Russian history, and the west door is dedicated to the lives of Sts Peter and Paul. The scenes on the panels are arranged in three successive planes; this helps to achieve a sense of deep space without destroying the plane of the door.

Great west inner
door. By Ivan Vitali.
1850. Oakwood and
bronze

Detail of decoration
of the drum of the
main dome

The Prophet Ezekiel.
Figure on a vault. By
Ivan Vitali. Copper
gilt (galvanoplasty).
1845-50

Methods of modelling and the workmanship standards indicate that the reliefs on the doors were executed by different hands. Vitali must have entrusted part of the work to his pupils.

The finest are the reliefs on the great west door. Depicted on the left fold are scenes of *The Conversion of St Paul on the Way to Damascus, St Paul Preaching Before the Areopagus at Athens, St Paul Before King Agrippa* and *The Martyrdom of St Paul.*

Among the finest decorations in the Cathedral are those on the drum of the main dome, which follow the general lines of the Renaissance style. Painted images of the Apostles alternate with statues of angels. The large windows admit plenty of light to play on the gilt angel figures, which provides for a striking effect.

On 30 May 1858 the Cathedral was finally opened. The consecration ceremony was attended by Alexander II and the imperial family, by high-placed dignitaries of the church and the court. Units of the Guards also took part in the ceremony. "Outsiders" were not admitted either into the Cathedral or into the adjacent area, but they could watch the event from the roofs of the nearby houses. The consecration of St Isaac's Cathedral was a striking manifestation of the league of the autocratic regime and the Russian Church.

Consecrated on that day (the 30th of May was the birthday of Peter the Great and St Isaac's feast day) was only the main sanctuary dedicated to St Isaac the Dalmatian. The chapel of St Catherine was consecrated on the following day, and that of St Alexander Nevsky on 7 July.

St Isaac's became the principal cathedral of the capital of the Russian Empire and an important centre of the Russian Orthodox Church.

After the 1917 October Revolution the Cathedral continued to operate (till 1928). In 1931, it was converted into a museum by a decree of the Soviet government. In the same year the well-known Soviet astronomer Nikolai Kamenshchikov staged in the museum the world's largest experiment with the Foucault pendulum; it demonstrated the earth's rotation on its axis, postulated by Copernicus. Today this experiment is demonstrated at the Leningrad Planetarium.

During the War of 1941-45 the Cathedral premises were used for storing treasures and archives brought there from several palace museums in the city's environs. Sculptures, furniture, porcelain and museum documents of the greatest value were carefully preserved by the museum's staff throughout the long and hard months of the Leningrad blockade by the army of Nazi Germany.

The Cathedral museum suffered heavy damage during the war years, particularly as regards its decoration. Large-scale restoration work conducted by many architects, artists and sculptors in the postwar period returned its former splendour to the Cathedral. This majestic edifice still sums up the achievements in building techniques, architecture and various branches of decorative art in Russia during the first half of the nineteenth century.

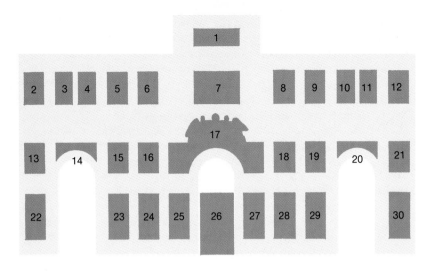

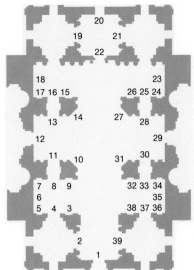

The Main Iconostasis

1. *The Agony in the Garden*
2. *The Patriarch Abraham*
3. *The Patriarch Melchizedek*
4. *King Solomon*
5. *The Prophet Elijah*
6. *The Prophet Daniel*
7. *The Last Supper*
8. *The Prophet Isaiah*
9. *The Prophet Jeremiah*
10. *King David*
11. *The Patriarch Noah*
12. *Adam the Forefather*
13. *St Prince Vladimir and St Princess Olga*
14. *The Tables of the Law*
15. *Mary Magdalen and Queen Alexandra*
16. *St Nicholas of Novgorod*
17. Sculptural group: *Christ in Majesty and Patriarchs, Forbears of the House of Romanov*
18. *The Archangel Michael*
19. *The Prophetess Anna and the Righteous Elizabeth*
20. *Life-giving Vessel*
21. *St Helena and St Constantine, Equal to the Apostles*
22. *The Apostle Paul*
23. *St Catherine*
24. *St Alexander Nevsky*
25. *The Virgin and Child*
26. The Holy Doors with the four Evangelists and the Annunciation
27. *The Saviour*
28. *St Isaac the Dalmatian*
29. *St Nicholas of Myra*
30. *The Apostle Peter*

The Attic: Murals and Mosaics

1. *The Creation of the World*
2. *The Flood*
3. *Moses*
4. *The Burning Bush*
5. *Moses and Aaron Before the Pharaoh*
6. *The Crossing of the Red Sea*
7. *The Song of Miriam*
8. *Moses Receives the Tables of the Law on Mt Sinai*
9. *The Commandment of Moses*
10. *The Scourging of Christ*
11. *The Parable of the Wedding Guests*
12. *The Feeding of the Five Thousand*
13. *The Parable of the Prodigal Son*
14. *The Betrayal*
15. *The Healing of the Blind Man*
16. *The Repenting Sinner*
17. *The Healing of the Paralytic*
18. *The Raising of the Widow's Son of Nain*
19. *The Appearance of Christ to the Apostles*
20. *The Incredulity of Thomas*
21. *The Washing of the Disciples' Feet*
22. *The Vernicle*
23. *The Raising of Lazarus*
24. *Christ Walking on the Waves*
25. *The Wedding at Cana*
26. *The Healing of the Leper*
27. *Christ Before Pilate*
28. *The Parable of the Good Samaritan*
29. *The Sermon on the Mount*
30. *The Parable of the Stealthy Sower*
31. *Christ Bearing the Cross*
32. *Aaron's Offering to the Lord*
33. *Joshua*
34. *Gideon's Fleece*
35. *Joseph Receives His Father and Brothers in Egypt*
36. *Jacob's Ladder*
37. *Isaac Blessing Jacob*
38. *Abraham's Sacrifice*
39. *The Sacrifice of Noah after the Flood*

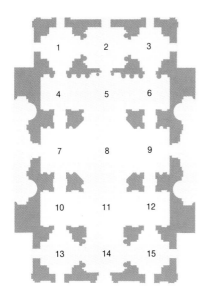

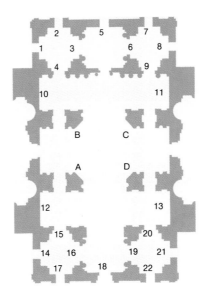

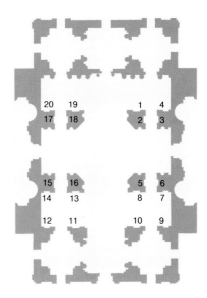

Ceiling

1. *Christ the Pantocrator Borne by Angels*
2. *The Only Begotten*
3. *The Assumption*
4. *Angels Bearing Scrolls with the Commandments*
5. *The Last Judgement*
6. *Angels Bearing Scrolls with the Commandments*
7. *Angels with a Chalice*
8. *The Virgin in Majesty*
9. *Angels with a Gospel Book*
10. *The Fiery Ascent of the Prophet Elijah*
11. *The Vision of the Prophet Ezekiel*
12. *The Prophet Enoch*
13. *Isaac the Dalmatian*
14. *The Creation of the Sun and the Moon*
15. *St Febronia*

Lunettes

1. *The Victory of Prince Alexander Nevsky over the Swedes*
2. *Prince Alexander Nevsky Praying Before the Cross for the Deliverance of His Homeland*
3. *The Death of Prince Alexander Nevsky*
4. *The Translation of the Relics of Prince Alexander Nevsky from Vladimir to St Petersburg in 1724*
5. *The Holy Spirit Surrounded by Angels*
6. *The Martyrdom of St Demetrius of Thessalonica*
7. *The Martyrdom of St Catherine*
8. *The Martyrdom of St George*
9. *St Barbara Renounces All Worldly Goods*
10. *Christ Blessing the Little Children*
11. *Christ in the House of Martha and Mary*
12. *The Death of the Firstborn in Egypt*
13. *Jacob Blessing the Sons of Joseph*
14. *The Baptism of Grand Prince Vladimir*
15. *Grand Prince Vladimir Chooses the Greek Church*
16. *The Baptism of the People in Kiev*
17. *Grand Prince Vladimir Cured of Blindness*
18. *God Blessing His Creation*
19. *The Icon of Our Lady of Kazan Before the Kremlin Walls at the time of the War with Napoleon in 1812*
20. *The Apostolic Council in Jerusalem*
21. *The Metropolitan Peter Giving His Blessing to Grand Prince Ivan of Moscow for the Building of a Stone Cathedral of the Dormition of the Virgin*
22. *St Sergius of Radonezh Blessing Grand Prince Dmitry Donskoi Before the Battle of Kulikovo*

Pendentives

A *St Luke the Evangelist*
B *St Matthew the Evangelist*
C *St Mark the Evangelist*
D *St John the Evangelist*

Paintings in the Niches of Piers

1. *The Presentation of the Virgin*
2. *The Descent of the Holy Spirit on the Apostles*
3. *The Ascension*
4. *The Nativity of the Virgin*
5. *The Presentation in the Temple*
6. *The Circumcision of Christ*
7. Exhibit missing
8. *The Ascension*
9. *The Nativity of John the Baptist*
10. *Joachim and Anne*
11. *The Baptism of Christ*
12. *The Nativity of the Virgin*
13. *The Resurrection*
14. *The Entry into Jerusalem*
15. *The Crucifixion*
16. *The Deposition*
17. *The Exaltation of the Cross*
18. *Jesus Sends the Napkin with the Imprint of His Image to Abgar of Edessa*
19. *The Dormition of the Virgin*
20. *The Intercession*

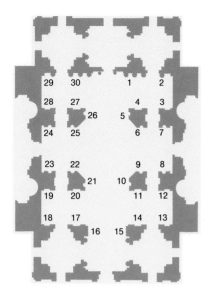

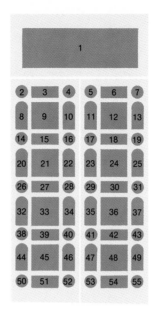

Sculptures on the Vaults

1. *The Apostle Trophimus*
2. *The Apostle Simeon Called Niger*
3. *The Apostle Joseph*
4. *The Apostle Simeon*
5. *The Archangel Michael*
6. *Angel of Salvation*
7. *Angel of Rejoicing*
8. *Guiding Angel*
9. *Angel of Concordance*
10. *Angel Salathiel*
11. *The Prophet Nathan*
12. *The Prophet Jesus, Son of Sirach*
13. *The Prophet Baruch*
14. *The Prophet Micah*
15. *Angel Praising the Creator*
16. *Angel Praising the Creator*
17. *The Prophet Ezekiel*
18. *The Prophet Elisha*
19. *The Prophet Amos*
20. *The Prophet Obadiah*
21. *The Archangel Uriel*
22. *Guardian Angel*
23. *Angel of Virtue*
24. *Angel of Faith*
25. *Angel of Repentance*
26. *The Archangel Gabriel*
27. *The Apostle Ananias*
28. *The Apostle Timothy*
29. *The Apostle Agabus*
30. *The Apostle Joseph*

Reliefs on the Great Inner Doors

West Door

1. *The Exaltation of the Cross*
2. *St Joachim*
3. *Angels Prospering the Way of a Saint*
4. *St Anne*
5. *St Zacharias*
6. *Angels Prospering the Way of a Saint*
7. *St Elizabeth*
8. *Simeon, the God-Receiver*
9. *The Conversion of St Paul on the Way to Damascus*
10. *The Prophetess Anna*
11. *Joseph, Husband of the Virgin*
12. *St Peter Confesses Jesus to Be the Christ*
13. *Cleopas, Brother of Joseph, Husband of the Virgin*
14. *Mary Magdalen*
15. *Mary, the Mother of James*
16. *Salome, the Holy Myrrhophore*
17. *Martha*
18. *Mary*
19. *Lazarus*
20. *St James the Great*
21. *St Paul Preaching Before the Areopagus at Athens*
22. *St Simon*
23. *St Joseph of Arimathaea*
24. *The Sermon of St Peter and the Descent of the Holy Spirit on the Apostles*
25. *St Nicodemus*
26. *Deacon Philip*
27. *Deacon Prochorus*
28. *Deacon Nicanor*
29. *Deacon Timon*
30. *Deacon Parmenas*
31. *Deacon Nicholas*
32. *St Stephen, the Protomartyr*
33. *St Paul Before King Agrippa*
34. *St Barnabas*
35. *Centurion Longinus*
36. *St Peter's Vision of Unclean Beasts*
37. *Centurion Cornelius*
38. *Herodion*

39. *Agabus*
40. *Rufus*
41. *Asyncritus*
42. *Phlegon*
43. *Hermes*
44. *St Clement the First*
45. *The Martyrdom of St Paul*
46. *Dionysius the Areopagite*
47. *St Ignatius Theophoros*
48. *The Martyrdom of St Peter*
49. *St Polycarp, Bishop of Smyrna*
50. *Angel Opening the Book of Acts of the Apostle Paul*
51. *St Sophia (Wisdom)*
52. *St Pistis (Faith)*
53. *St Elpis (Hope)*
54. *Angel Opening the Book of Acts of the Apostle Peter*
55. *St Agape (Charity)*

North Door

1. *Christ Explains the Images on the Silver Piece*
2. *St Antony the Great*
3. *Angels Prospering the Way of a Saint*
4. *St Paul the Hermit*
5. *St Macarius of Egypt*
6. *Angels Prospering the Way of a Saint*
7. *St Macarius of Alexandria*
8. *St Constantine*
9. *The Meeting Between St Isaac the Dalmatian and the Emperor Valens*
10. *St Helena*
11. *The Martyr George*
12. *St Nicholas the Miracle Worker Is Ordained Hierodeacon*
13. *Warrior John, the Great Martyr*
14. *St Pachomius*
15. *St Arsenius*
16. *St Euthymius*
17. *St Hilarion*
18. *St Humphrey*
19. *St Peter of Athos*
20. *St Gregory of Caesarea*
21. *St Isaac the Dalmatian Delivered by Angels from the Swamp*
22. *St Cyprian, Bishop of Carthage*
23. *St Athanasius the Great*
24. *St Nicholas the Miracle Worker*
25. *St Cyril of Alexandria*
26. *St Catherine the Martyr*
27. *St Barbara the Martyr*
28. *St Alexandra the Martyr*
29. *St Febronia the Martyr*
30. *St Macrina the Younger, Sister of Basil the Great*
31. *St Nonna, Mother of Gregory the Theologian*
32. *St Cyril of Jerusalem*
33. *St Isaac the Dalmatian Released from the Dungeon*
34. *St Basil the Great*
35. *St Gregory the Theologian*
36. *St Nicholas the Miracle Worker Elected Archbishop of Myra in Lycia*
37. *St John Chrysostom*
38. *St Agathonicus the Martyr*
39. *St Cosmas the Miracle Worker*
40. *St Damian the Miracle Worker*
41. *St Theodore Stratilates the Martyr*
42. *St Florus the Martyr*
43. *St Laurus the Martyr*
44. *St Spiridion of Tremithus*
45. *St Theodosius Blessed by St Isaac the Dalmatian*
46. *St Gregory of Nicae*
47. *St Epiphanius, Bishop of Cyprus*
48. *St Nicholas the Miracle Worker Disgraces Arius at the General Council*
49. *St Ambrose of Mediolanum*
50. *Deaconess Theoseblia, Wife of Gregory of Nyssa*

51. *Angel Opening the Book of Acts of Isaac the Dalmatian*
52. *St Irene the Martyr*
53. *St Theodora the Martyr*
54. *Angel Opening the Book of Acts of St Nicholas the Miracle Worker*
55. *St Didymus the Warrior*

South Door

1. *The Consecration of the Temple of Jerusalem*
2. *St Methodius*
3. *Angels Prospering the Way of a Saint*
4. *St Cyril*
5. *St Antony of the Caves (Pechersky)*
6. *Angels Prospering the Way of a Saint*
7. *St Theodosius of the Caves (Pechersky)*
8. *Michael, First Metropolitan of Kiev*
9. *Philosopher Teaching Christianity to Prince Vladimir*
10. *St Olga*
11. *St Boris*
12. *The Victory of Prince Alexander Nevsky over the Swedes*
13. *St Gleb*
14. *St Michael of Murom*
15. *St Constantine of Murom*
16. *St Theodore*
17. *St David of Yaroslavl*
18. *St Theodore of Smolensk and Yaroslavl*
19. *St Constantine of Yaroslavl*
20. *Peter, Metropolitan of Kiev*
21. *Prince Vladimir Listens to the Judgements of His Counsellors about the Different Religions*
22. *St Alexius, Metropolitan of Moscow*
23. *Jonas, Metropolitan of Moscow*
24. *Prince Alexander Nevsky Rejects the Proposal of Pope Innocent IV that He Convert to the Western Church*
25. *St Philip, Metropolitan of Moscow*
26. *St Sergius of Radonezh*
27. *St Cyril of Lake Beloye*
28. *Euthymius of Suzdal*
29. *St Paphnutius of Borovsk*
30. *St Barlaam of Khutyn*
31. *St Nicholas the Miracle Worker of Novgorod*
32. *St George, Son of Prince Vsevolod*
33. *The Baptism of Prince Vladimir*
34. *Vsevolod, Son of Prince Mstislav of Kiev*
35. *St Theodore, Son of Prince Yaroslav*
36. *Prince Alexander Nevsky Takes Monastic Vows*
37. *St Daniel, Son of Prince Alexander Nevsky*
38. *St Michael, Prince of Chernigov*
39. *The Boyar Theodore*
40. *St Demetrius*
41. *Nicholas, Prince of Chernigov, Called the Bigot*
42. *St John, Prince of Uglich*
43. *Peter, Tsarevich of the Horde*
44. *St Stephen, Bishop of Perm*
45. *Prince Vladimir Baptizes the People of Kiev*
46. *St Innocent, Bishop of Irkutsk*
47. *St Demetrius, Metropolitan of Rostov*
48. *The Translation of the Relics of Alexander Nevsky from Vladimir to St Petersburg in 1724*
49. *St Metrophanes, Bishop of Voronezh*
50. *Euphrosyne of Polotsk*
51. *Angel Opening the Book of Acts of St Vladimir*
52. *Euphrosyne of Suzdal*
53. *St Peter, Prince of Murom*
54. *Angel Opening the Book of Acts of St Alexander Nevsky*
55. *St Febronia*